Alcohol

THE SLOW KILL

Mark Holmes

PAGE PUBLISHING
Conneaut Lake, PA

First originally published by Page Publishing 2022

ISBN 978-1-6624-7539-9 (pbk)
ISBN 978-1-6624-7540-5 (digital)

Printed in the United States of America

L ook at me, the way I live, the money I have, you see the difference in you and me is that I'm an alcoholic, but you are a drunk; there's a difference Right. I once said that to a guy, and I Really believed that…until.

It's been what seemed to be a lifetime ago when I took my first drink of alcohol, I was 19 years old at a disco club. My first was rum and coke mixed in a full glass with ice. A double shot at that time cost $1.75 cents and two of them would carry me through the time I was there.

In those days I didn't drink to get drunk and being buzzed wasn't what I had in mind, for me it was an image thing, what I did to make myself look good to the girls. Swagging around the club, cup in hand looking to be seen,1983.

My club nights were on Friday, and Saturday, the rest of the week alcohol never crossed my mind. Those were the days.

I celebrated New Year's Eve 1984, drinking a different brand of alcohol because by then, I no longer had a taste for the mix. My new choice was "Paul Mason" with a glass of coke on the side, no ice. That was my year of lifestyle change; the year my alcohol-use became experimental. The year I changed from drinking to look good, to wanting that buzz, and that was the beginning of what I now realize to be *the slow kill.*

Unlike others my age, I didn't have a nine-to-five job. My mother taught me how to make money legally, she introduced me to real estate business. Buying, fixing up houses and selling them; she also taught me to use common sense as a foundation when making decisions in life, and to be self-motivated but more importantly, independent. I took her words to heart as a young man and made money…my way. She introduced me to people who own real estate and construction companies; and by associating with them I further my financial independent way of thinking. Basically, when I woke up in the morning, my day was mine. I was on my own.

In 1984, life was good. Through my association with these self-made men, I obtained my second property and was establishing myself financially in construction business. They would meet at restaurants on certain weekdays, usually around one or two o'clock late afternoon or seven, at times eight o'clock in the evening. They called them *"meets"*. The conversation was strictly money. How to make it, how to spend it, who brought what or how somebody was to invest in something. I remember during one of those *"meets"* I commented *"I learn so much from y'all when we meet like this, then one of them responded* half-drunk red eyed with a cheesy smile on his face *"yeah young holmes, the way you keep learning kid you'll be richer than me one day, saying: just call this a meeting of the minds"*. The four of them looked at me, heads gesturing approval laughing as they raised their glasses in a toasting his comments.

There was always liquor at the meet's, drinking alcohol was always at the center of it all, and they would drink the strong stuff, expensive and always "straight up". That means with no mix no chaser just alcohol; and I would hear everything, see every expression, every gesture; and it didn't take long for me to follow suit.

I was 22 years old and to me alcohol became a status symbol, a sign of success. To me this is what businesspeople who make money does, that this is a part of being rich. But I was a young man making money and my inexperience caused me to make bad choices. I learned later in life that having money does not qualify a person as brilliant. But I was making it every day, my way, with no one questioning my decisions or directly over seeing my choices.

As the 80s progressed my alcohol use was becoming a routine, and I was unconsciously becoming a "functioning alcoholic". I didn't see it. I never paid that a thought, partly because it had no noticeable effect on my ability to make money, my day-to-day lifestyle, or sport activities I engaged in. I would go about my life not realizing the mental and physical effect that was creeping behind me, or the dark path of consequences my use of alcohol set in motion.

["a functioning alcoholic is often in denial because to admit that is to admit failure."] (C.D.C.P.) ["In the United States, the ("Center for Disease Control & Prevention) also known as the C.D.C.P, reported that 72 percent of Americans are functioning alcoholics". "That accounts for 17 million or more individuals, made up of men, women and youth however, because most functional alcoholics are in denial and do not seek help that number is more than likely higher."]

By the spring of 1985, I started a different kind of business, called "Production, or Promotions". I was now in the entertainment business giving parties and caberades for teenagers and young adults. These functions were promoted by passing out flyers, for teenage events I would advertise at high schools during the afternoon and when the school day ended around three o'clock. For adults, my advertisement would take place at night going to bars, clubs and cabarets given by other promoters. Promoting this way would take me all over the city of Cleveland, during the day from one high school to another; and at night to clubs and bars; and this kind of business allowed me what I would call, open freedom. What I mean by that is no encounters with people who wore suits and ties, and this changed my lifestyle. It created a different routine for me. Those days of drinking only on Friday and Saturday night and sit down meets at restaurants with the realtors and investors, were a thing of the past.

I acquired a new timeline for alcohol drinking that started at 12 noon, throughout the afternoon and into the night. My new lifestyle also changes my choice of liquors, let me explain. My associates were no longer realtors and construction company owners, they were now people who live the night life. I was now dealing with a different type of associates, most of them were past or active criminals, drug dealers, addicts, killers and thieves, but 90 percent of them had one thing in common which was either drugs or alcohol abusers: in most cases both.

Outside of the building owners I would meet with to rent their venue for my events, my new associates were not the sit down at a restaurant type of drinker, or the sipping type, and definitely not into the expensive alcohol brands. They drank the brands that would guarantee a right to the point high, there was no getting buzzed, just head banging "tore up from the floor up" "feeling no pain" drunk, and by 1987, I was in the mix with several new afternoon and nighttime drinks.

I no longer had a taste for a specific brand, it was no longer about looking good for the girls or wanting to be seen. I drank for one purpose and my choice of liquors spoke that loud and clear. They were "*Mad Dog 20-20, Orange Jubilee*" and the granddaddy of them all, "*Wild Irish Rose*" all guaranteed to put an elephant on its ass. But that wasn't good enough for me so I went extreme by mixing them together one with another or occasionally all three in one glass; doing this would cause the heaviest drinkers give me a glare, even known drunks would look at me and shake their head, and others even while drunk would take a step away.

I was still going out to bars; still clubbing, but like my afternoon choices I no longer had a specific brand. My choice now was any alcohol, dark or white. I didn't care as long as it was as close to 100 proof as possible. I can remember times when I would mix dark liquor in the same glass as white, it didn't matter to me as long as I got drunk. I remember stopping at after hour joints when the bars would close, buying and mixing anything they had left in one large cup. I would even buy and throw moonshine in the mix.

But throughout the mid-eighties I was still a social drinker, the type who would sit down, drink and conversate. Talk to the girls laugh and joke; the type who would be there until the bar stop serving. I can't remember a time not hearing "*last call for alcohol*", and I was always "the last man standing". Those words, "*Last call*" were sad to my ears, but I knew it was coming, at some point the place has to close but I didn't fret about it, not at all because I had a backup plan you see, I always kept a bottle stashed in my glove compartment.

"A U D" also known as Alcohol Use Disorder", defined in layman terms: a person who will not stop drinking until he or she pass out". I want you to really understand what this means. It is not saying (**run out of liquor**) but **literally pass out**. "This behavior can be found in both anti-social and social alcoholics". These are the people who **cannot** have a bar in their home because they will drink non-stop until all the liquor is either gone or they pass out, and there is no **"order"** in this behavior.

People who know me know that when it came to food, I love to eat, you name it, if it's edible I'm eating it. I was once told by a friend, *"Mark, you spend your money on two things, food and clothes". My best friend Joe words which to this day are true, "Mark you'll either be fat and rich or skinny and poor."* I laughed when they said these things but as the years passed, I began to understand how seriously right they were. "Alcohol flows through the blood system to the stomach and small intestine; then circulates throughout a person's system." (C.D.C.P.) and this for me, also contributed to a loss appetite leading to what I call *The Slow Kill,* and in time, I became a billboard for such behavior.

I was allowing alcohol a place in my life, but wasn't satisfied with just drinking, I wanted to get higher, so in 1987 I welcome other drugs into my world. Drugs like Marijuana and "PCP", which is a liquid acid. Most people use this by dipping a cigarette, or a marijuana joint into the liquid substance until it drips wet, then when it dries, smoke it. I did that, but thirst for more. So, I started using powder cocaine, which was quickly followed by crack rock cocaine. The crack was seriously addictive and affected me in the worst way. I was strung out and using every trick in the book to feed that addiction, but during that madness and all the drama it brought into my life, I never gave up my first love, *alcohol.*

As bad as these drugs were, I consider them to be slight additions; I say slight because they were short lived compared to my alcohol abuse. They were "chasers", for example, ordering a drink of alcohol with a beer or soda on the side, and although they affected my life in a bad way the history was short-lived.

I used the substance "PCP" for about two months but quickly stopped because it made my mind and actions ridiculously crazy.

One incident that stands out in my mind became *"the straw that broke the camel's back,"* I remember this like it was yesterday. Summertime Mid July. It was hot during the day, clear and warm at night. I had been passing out flyers for an upcoming party, drinking and smoking pcp all afternoon and into the night, and was beyond high. I think it was about ten o'clock at night, maybe eleven I'm not sure because I was so high. But This guy I knew said to me *"Mark, the club on "such and such" street is packed; you can get a lot of flyers off"*. Now one thing about me back then, was that high or higher, I would not lose focus on my goal at hand. So, we went there, and I'm inside this bar passing out flyers, smoking more PCP and drinking really cheap but hard cord liquor; and at some point, I must have gone to the bathroom, but I don't remember going, but that is where I woke up, dazed and confused. At first, I thought it was a dream. It wasn't. My head was spinning. I walked out and to the main door, pushed it, and quickly realized that I was locked in. The bar was closed for the night, and I was locked in. I figured while closing they missed me when I was in the bathroom stall paralyzed, probably because they were high too. My body had shut down while I was in the bathroom.

"PCP" has such a bad effect on the body that if you smoke too much of it or dip too heavy in the liquid acid, that while smoking the body will shut down to protect itself, and you will literally freeze where you stand or sit.

I walked around trying to get out, and as my senses begin to kick in; I fully realized this dilemma. Well, to make a long story short I managed to get out of the bar undetected. Somewhat panicked I broke the side door open and left, the alarm was going off but of course I managed to grab two bottles of "Martel" for the road, but after that situation I promptly ended that relationship.

I will be brief about me and powder cocaine which wasn't a good relationship, because it distorted my alcohol taste buds and that alone was a problem. The combination gave me a headache and then there was the runny and sore nose from snorting. I would throw up my alcohol and have the worst case of diarrhea. Putting it in a cigarette didn't help, doing that made my mouth chalky and the alcohol felt heavy going down my throat; on top of all that, it sobers me up faster than I wanted to be. I was not going to allow that to happen, so after one month it had to go!

My two-time addiction to crack cocaine is an embarrassing story for another time, but I'll say this, my first round ended with me having doubt that it was stronger than me, then after a few years past I went for round two, but after that two-month heavyweight championship battle, I lost in a shameful fashion. I was forced to admit defeat and bow out with what I had left of my self-esteem, and like a wounded animal ran away with my tail between my legs as far as I could get. I never challenged it again.

I am sure as you're reading, you're wondering, what about the Marijuana, what happened with that? The answer to that is, *and then there were three.*

So now my life consists of Alcohol, Marijuana, and Black & Mild Cigars, so what Mark has brought together let no man, or God pull apart.

Sex was never that important to me, I was never the type of man who "had to have it" and didn't pursue it, but somehow would happen be in the right place at the right time. Now don't get the wrong impression, I enjoy having sex, but for me, the excitement was in the mental challenge "*the game*", me versus her and the words used that led to the prize, my excitement was in the chase.

I remember my first sexual experience when I was young and sober. It was 1983 in the backseat of my car with a street walker aka prostitute.

She was my first and I went that route although there were women who knew me and wanted to go the distance. but because I was popular, I feared that being a virgin if my performance would not stand up to my hipe and if that got out it would ruin my reputation. So, I called myself paying for training. However, things did not go over as I planned because as soon as she touched my you know what and was putting it you know where, let's just say the training cost me fifty bucks and lasted maybe thirty seconds and never reached the destination. I asked for a second round, but she wanted another fifty bucks. I declined, but learn one thing, that there has to be a better way. I was sober that night so long ago, but what I didn't realize was that the next time I would have a sober sexual experience would be 38 years in the future.

I was 19 years old at that time and after that fiasco, over the course of years I've met and had sex with several women. It has been said that "sex to some is like a drug", and in an odd way it became like that for me, but like the other drugs I once used, it also became a chaser to my alcohol addiction. To say it bluntly, if I wasn't drinking, if there was no alcohol, I had no interest in having sex, and as the years pasted my alcohol abuse got so bad that I no longer fear what a woman would think or say if my sexual performance was bad, my fear was if I could perform without being under the influence.

Throughout the 1990s, and into the 2000's, alcohol was a controlling factor in my life. However, that is not how I saw it, or maybe I didn't want to see it. The "*slow kill*" was controlling my mind, body and spirit. A friend once said to me "*Mark, I will tell you the biggest problem people have when it comes to smoking and why it's hard to stop, we developed a habit, for example, smoke after we eat, smoke after sex, while driving, and after a task.* I have found that to be a similarity when it comes to alcohol use and how that can easily become a habit. For example, a drink comes before dinner and after, a drink after work. Alcohol before and after sex, drinking at parties, family and friend outings and even at funeral bypasses, but when the combination of marijuana and alcohol use becomes a habit, that is when it becomes dangerous, and for me, her words became biblical.

Throughout the late 90s into the early 2000 my alcoholism was now routine. It was now a habit, and my life became as the saying goes "*same old same old*". But during the years of 2000 through 2005, there was a change in my life, I was in a relationship raising her kids. Going to school events, parent-teacher meetings, doing the family thing. I really enjoyed that period in my life; being the father figure changed the way I looked at a lot of things. It changed the way I thought about things and how I carried myself. I matured; even got out of the promotion business and back into real estate and construction. Gone was the nightlife, the bars and clubs' things were different now, well, kinda.

I mean, my drinking was still my drinking, but I somewhat changed my routine during that relationship. I no longer started drinking in the afternoon, only in the evenings, well, sometimes but that was good right? Wait, before you agree because I must admit that when I got off work, I did make up that non-drinking time and would start up as I drove home, and yea throughout the night until I passed out. But I was able to control the amount I would drink on school event evenings. Then again yeah, once home I would make up for that time too. When I think back about it one thing was accomplished for sure, I had finally become a full-blown "functioning alcoholic". I was hiding my abuse, living this double lifestyle, drinking as it's called "*in the closet*". No one in the outside world knew that I was a drunk, but that success came with consequences because I didn't live with the people in the outside world and could not hide this disease from the people inside my world. The drinking caused mood swings, arguments, lies, and bad decisions that ended that relationship that led to me once again, being on my own.

That was many years ago, but even today I often reflect on those years. Her kids are grown with kids of their own and I have no relationship with them. In my heart I know that my alcoholism played a part in the breakdown of what could have been a good thing, and for some men, that would have made them re-evaluate alcohol and marijuana abuse and its cause and effect. But that would be for some men.

I was single again going out to clubs; back at bars living the nightlife; making decisions that I selfishly thought only affected me, but I was wrong. In 1999 I relocated from Cleveland Ohio to Detroit Michigan, leaving behind family and friends I had known for decades. I could talk with most of them about anything and they would listen to everything. I was considered family, welcomed into their homes, trusted buy them and their kids. It was no surprise to anyone who knew me that I drank. Throughout my years living in Cleveland, I would attend holiday affairs, birthday parties and weddings where alcohol was a normal feature; We all knew each other and was there to laugh, talk and have fun; while there, our drinking went unnoticeable, we were amongst family and at such functions as long as there was no crazy outburst it was acceptable to get *so call "tipsy"*. In those days I was still considered a "sociable drinker", but I wasn't, not at all. Back then I was a heavy closet drinker.

There were some "who had a feeling", however, because I never acted as an out of control drunk, those that had a feeling would let the thought pass; and that controlled drinking ability, allow me to hide my dark secret.

After I moved from Ohio, there would be times when someone coming to Detroit, either by themself or with family called me asking if they could stop by to see me, or meet up with me at one of the summer festivals, a restaurant or club. I would respond with one of my pre-rehearsed lies so they wouldn't see my weight loss or the red eye sick look that constant drinking gives a person. I would lie that I'm not in town, although they gave me advance notice that they were coming. That lie would come with a short story attached and became my go to lie because it could cover a period of days just in case their visit was prolonged and using it was better than just not answering the phone call.

I had so many excuses when asked to come visit Cleveland Ohio it was pitiful. I would be invited to a high-school graduation or weddings. Even when one of their kids I use to play with now a teenager would go out their way to invite me to their birthday party, I'd lie. It didn't matter to me I had something for everything. I would lie yes at times, going as far as giving a date of my arrival and not show up; I would get creative too, and here are a few of my best:

This one was good, my lie that I am so busy with all this work that just happened to come about, or that I had to handle family affairs although that relationship ended years ago, I had no family; then there was the one about me all of a sudden having to go to the hospital because of some illness I would make up that just happened to befall me the night before I was to arrive there.

Some lies were shameful, among the worst was claiming that a family member just had a heart attack and suddenly died, all the while I'm sitting there drinking, telling lies drunk as they give me their sympathy. I was pathetic. However, for those who lived in Detroit who would invite me to a gathering, a sport event or barbeque, I had lies for them too. My go to lie was that my back is hurting so bad I can't move, straining the tone in my voice like I'm trying to win an academy award. That lie was told for daytime events; For nighttime affairs, I would say that I can't see driving at night or that I just took medication, and my head is throbbing. That lie was said to people who would say "Mark I can come pick you up" when the truth of the matter was that I had become an "Anti-Social drinker" who was either drinking or already drunk which was what I did all the time. No one ever outright confronted or challenge my reasons; they didn't know that I was an alcoholic; They could not imagine me having that kind of weakness. The Mark Holmes they know was a man in complete control of his life, but I was weak, weaken by the alcohol disease and trapped in my own lies. I needed my lies to be their reality, so I stuck with it and double down on them. By 2006, 2007 I had told too many lies to so many people I felt no way out. I felt that there was no way to redeem myself, no turning back as I stayed on this alcoholic path to destruction.

When that relationship ended around 2005, my old drinking routines came back on steroids.

By 2008 my life was routine, I would wake up and go to sleep drinking. Drinking was my routine, my habit and became my life-style, and for those who consider drinking a celebration then I celebrated. I celebrated waking up in the morning. Turning on the TV was a celebration. I celebrated driving and using the toilet, I celebrate before sex, during and after, I even celebrated celebrating. You remembered that guy "Grady" who was on the TV show "Sanford and Son", the one who would raise his glass to anything saying, "I'll drink to that", I became him constantly raising my bottle killing myself. But unlike that tv show my abuse was real, and I wasn't funny.

I didn't eat lunch, I drank it, alcohol was my ride alone friend and I celebrated going to, during and from work. My celebrating had got to a point where I didn't drink alcohol with my dinner alcohol was my dinner. I pulled into more liquor stores than fast food joints; order more bottles than hamburgers, put more liquor in my stomach than chicken wings, everyday all day this was my life but there was a time I didn't drink, that would usually happen around the end of the night when I would pass out drunk which was a regular routine as well. Drinking three to four pints of liquor everyday throughout the day tends to have that effect. I would usually pass out around ten or eleven o'clock at night, and the good thing about passing out was that I would never be able to finish that 4th pint. There would always be some left until I woke up about three, four or five o'clock the next morning, and when I did the celebration would continue. I can't say it start because the drinking never stopped, only a pause.

In a "CDCP" report they found that "high functioning alcoholics are often in denial because to admit to the disease is to admit to failure, however, the percentage of people that fall under this category is not clear because most do not seek help." it added that "high functioning alcoholics have the ability to blend into society, holding jobs and families, socializing with friends, attending social events, living a similar lifestyle of non-alcoholics".

"I could walk through water and not get wet", "leap tall buildings in a single bound", "faster than a local motive". a Superman so I would say laughing, drunk bragging to others of my super ability to drive drunk and never get pulled over, or my inner powers that made me not have hangovers. I would say that alcohol doesn't affect me when I work, look at me, I'm still making money. However, that was not reality.

The reality was "dumb luck"; you see, my life consisted of two things: drinking and work.

By 2012, I stopped going to clubs and bars and because of my lying excuses, no one invited me to their social functions. Those days were gone; There were no more requests from Cleveland Ohio to visit and only one person would occasionally call to say hi.

I managed to cut everyone off and successfully became an "anti-social drunk" who did 80% of my drinking at home. I would end my workday no later than four, or five o'clock, and head home; that's where I would be, therefore my super ability to have never gotten pulled over for drunk driving was not super at all, it was because I was in my house by sunset; never stepping out at night when most drinkers get pulled over for driving drunk. In reality my superpower was actually having no life, just a bottle and boredom. Now as for my inner power to consume all that alcohol and never have hangovers well, there is a reason for that as well. As I said I would drink until I passed out and as soon as my eyes opened so did the bottle with the leftover liquor, so the real secret behind that ability was that I would never stop drinking; never gave my brain an opportunity to start its healing process and having a hangover is part of the healing. Therefore, the truth is that I did not have hangovers because I would not stop drinking. So no, I didn't have superpowers, no inner abilities, and honestly, me still being around to talk about this is luck, "dumb luck."

According to a "C.D.C. P" report "more than 95,000 people die each year from alcohol abuse, however that number is based on what is reported and is likely much higher". It defined heavy drinking as "8 or more drinks per week for women and 15 or more drinks per week for men".

They broke that down saying, "one shot of alcohol is considered a drink".

There are four shots in a half pint of liquor; eight shots equal one pint so modestly for a woman as stated by the "C.D.C. P". That would be one pint per week but keep in mind that their report uses the words [or more].

I personally as many of you, know women that drink more than that per week but let's move on. Their report states that for men 15 drinks [or more] per week is considered a heavy drinker which modestly amounts to roughly two pints per week. Now I'm not arguing their report, but I will say that maybe the next time they put their numbers together they should walk through my neighborhood.

By 2016, I was drinking four pints of liquor per day which doesn't include the times I would go to a liquor store that did not have my choice brand; when that happened, I would buy a shot bottle of a different liquor just to tie me over while I drive one or two blocks to the next store. You see, when I walk into a liquor store to buy my drink, I'm going to walk out with something, never nothing whether it is what I want or not. Therefore, when I add those shots into my regular consumption it rises to five pints per day; that adds up to 40 shots of liquor consumed by me per day, and two hundred shots over a period of 5 days.

Monday through Friday were my workdays, and I would take Saturday and Sunday off, those were considered my days of rest; on those days I did nothing physically, no work or lifting, except a minimum of six pints per day over that two-day period with the combination of marijuana being stuffed into my black & mild cigars. I will let you do the math because as I write I realize how lucky I am to be alive.

It was the summer of 2017, I came home from work at my usual time 4:30, or 5 o'clock, but on this day I wasn't feeling well, my body had an empty feel to it, I felt tired as if I had no energy, but did what I have been doing for decades, sat in my chair, turned on the TV, pulled out my bag of marijuana and started taking the tobacco out the black & mild cigar so I can stuff it with marijuana. That is how I smoked it.

I still had a half pint of liquor left from what I was drinking throughout the day; and of course on my way home although feeling ill I bought a fresh pint, with an additional shot to drink because I didn't want to open the fresh pint until I showered.

The half I had left I saved to make sure I would have something when I woke up from passing out, but when I puffed my marijuana cigar the smoke wouldn't go down my throat that felt like it was close.

I remember saying to myself, woe as I touched my swollen neck, but me being me my response to this unusual situation was to put the cigar down and pick up the liquor. I took a gop but like the smoke my throat would not allow it to digest.

I knew that something serious was going on here and began to debate with myself about what to do about this. The debate was about going to the hospital where they may keep me, and I can't drink versus, trying another way to get this marijuana and alcohol in my body; Yes, I was that bad. I was arguing with myself about either going to the hospital or taking a break from this decade's long ritual.

I decided to try smaller sips, and when the alcohol managed to drip down my throat, my decision was to wait until tomorrow to see if I feel better. I mean as long as I can get the alcohol in my body this swollen neck can wait, but as I consumed these drips, I started feeling a tightness in my chest, then realized that the alcohol was stopping there and not moving through my system.

I felt like I was drowning in the liquor as it sat at my chest starting to choke me, so I jumped up and ran into the bathroom, now looking in the mirror at my neck and seeing how blown up it was. My chest felt heavy; I needed to get this liquor out, so I grabbed a toothbrush, bent over the toilet and stuck it down my throat to throw up, and what came out was pure alcohol relieving my chest and stomach. My neck was sore and in pain. my chest felt heavy, sore and tight. I felt sick, my eyes bloodshot and water, but the thought of not drinking over weigh all of that. So, I went back into my living room, sat in my chair, raised my bottle and took a smaller sip, then another, but before I could take a third my heart started pounding harder than I ever felt; My chest tighten so tight I could barely breath, then I reluctantly put the bottle down and dialed 911.

The operator kept me on the phone as the ambulance raced to my house; I am very glad she did because with all that was happening to me, my thoughts were still on taking one more sip before they arrived. In my drug and alcohol induced mind I figured; well, the ambulance is coming so even if I come close to dying, they will bring me back to life.

Now hospitalized with i.v in both arms, a tube down my throat pumping alcohol from my body, I can't remember when I fell asleep, but I woke up the next afternoon very hungry; that is when I realized I had not eaten in over a week, and that I was in a near death situation.

Being in the hospital over a period of three days allowed me time to reflect on the actions that put me in that position. But it only took two days for me to remember that I spent almost a week prior to being hospitalized not eating or drinking water, just smoking marijuana, cigars and passing out drunk; even still I thought to myself that I've done nothing different than what I've been doing for decades, and eating very little over a period of time well, I've do that too; then it hit me, I haven't used the bathroom in a week, no bowel movement, no urinating. This is unlike before where the marijuana would make me eat something, and this time I haven't drank any water. My mind thought about that saying, "what goes in will come out". I have not put nothing solid in, only alcohol. My body had enough of that crap and started shutting itself down to protect itself. I guess when God created us humans, he was smart enough to give us more than one brain.

After two days the doctor came into my room, "Mr. Holmes, how do you feel"? with a soft relaxing tone, but I noticed no smile. "Mr. Holmes you suffered from alcohol poisoning, dehydration, and possibly a kidney issue"; we are going to do more testing and look at your lungs as well". But by this time, I was feeling better, extremely hungry so asked her if I could eat something? She replied "well, food in your system will offset the testing, but when we're done with that you can". I calmly said ok, although inside, my mind was racing and my stomach growling. At this point it has been roughly 9 days since I have chewed on solid food. They have only allowed me ice water. While still in the room she added, "Mr. Holmes, I want you to understand that this was a close call", "alcohol especially the amount we removed isn't good for you, as much as you have been drinking isn't good for anyone. I strongly recommend that you stop drinking any kind of alcohol" then with a serious look in her eyes her tone sharpen, "beer, wine at this point even a cooler will bring you right back here if you're lucky; or worst kill you". After saying that she turned and walked away.

Day four came on a Sunday and at this point the ice water wasn't cutting it, my hunger had me on edge and for the first time in a long time, I wanted food, to hell with alcohol. I needed to feel something in my belly, steaks, and fried chicken was on my mind. I needed to chew something, anything, even a stick of gum would bring satisfaction; besides that, all I could think about was this test the doctor mentioned, thinking to myself that after it, I can eat. So, with iv in my arm, using a walker I'm at the nurse desk. Excuse me, do you know when they will be doing the testing? She looked up glancing at me "oh no Mr. Holmes, they haven't called yet, but I'll call them and let you know". feeling helpless and hungry I turned and strolled back to my room. Twenty minutes passed as I made my way back to her desk, excuse me, has the doctor responded yet? This time in an irritated tone "no not yet Mr. Holmes".

My first approach was 7am that morning, my mouth was watering from hearing the sound of the plates, and the clanging noise of pan tops being lifted. The smell of eggs and toast was overwhelming; that was then at breakfast. Now it's 11:30. I looked out my room at the beef and rice being taken into the rooms of those sick lucky dogs; this was unbearable, so I had to ask the nurse a second time and after being told "no" I responded looking her in the eyes, if this testing doesn't happen by one o'clock, I'm checking myself out of this place; then walked away. I wanted the test I really did, but the hunger had me where I couldn't wait any more, I just couldn't take it.

At one o'clock, I made my last approach and asked for the last time, do you know what time the testing will be? "No Mr. Holmes we haven't heard from the Doctor yet". I calmly walked back to the room, removed the iv and took the back staircase out of the hospital and across the street to McDonald's.

The tone in my voice was desperate "a big Mac combo please, large, and a filet of fish sandwich. Oh miss, add an apple pie with that, two of them". My mouth was watering in anticipation of eating, my palms sweating, I can't wait to get this food in my stomach; from there to the gas station, "sir may I help you" I responded yes, five black & mild cigars. I spent almost twenty dollars on food alone and sat in the gas station parking lot eating.

My stomach was full and thoughts of going back to the hospital crossed my mind, but another thought filled my head also; I went with the latter. Looking across the street there's a cab in the hospital parking lot. I walked over to him asking, are you working? He responded "yes" I told him my address then slid inside. As he drove, I told him to make one stop before we get to my house, then motioned there, over there, and as he pulled over, I said "hey give me a second I won't be long, I just need to pick up a little something from this liquor store.

What I experienced that night, the pain, and that close call, was a first time for me; that doctor, that conversation those words was a first time for me. My stomach pumping, drinking that ice water, and feeling that helpless was a first time for me. the chest pain, that shortness of breath, that near death experience was a first time for me, but it would not be my last.

"Alcoholism is a Disease/ a Disorder, with long term effects to the brain and nervous system, heart, liver, and pancreas causing an increased blood pressure, high cholesterol levels ultimately bringing on strokes and heart attacks."

"Long term abuse can cause cancer of the liver, kidney, mouth, tongue—throat, esophagus and stomach." [United States C.D.C.P report]

Throughout the years I have had the best conversations with my oldest sister Joann. We would sit for hours and talk about all kinds of things, she would tell me stories about places, people and situations, things that have happened to her in life.

Her stories would make me laugh while others feel sad. The really funny ones would be about our relatives, situations they were in but especially the things they have said. One that stands out in my mind is about my Aunt Sara, she passed away many years ago, but if she was alive her age would be late 90ties.

My Aunt Sara was a drinker, and my sister would tell me stories of her hardships growing up. Explaining various circumstances that played a part in her alcoholism. "Mark, she said, talking about my aunt, "I'll never forget this. One night your Aunt Sara had been drinking, she was tore up laying on the couch falling to sleep, when her girlfriend Shirley came into the living room; she asked your aunt to hold some money for her and left out. Now your aunt Sara woke up surprised and happy about having this money, and she looked at me and said Joann, go to the liquor store and buy me a half gallon of vodka; and buy you some shoes, so I did and bought it back to her. I'm sitting there; Shirley comes back and asked, "Sara what happened to the money I told you to hold for me? Your aunt Sara asked her "was I drunk when you told me to hold some money"? Shirley said "yes", then your aunt Sara said, "well that's the problem".

My sister told me that story because when I'm drunk, I have a tendency of making promises and forgetting that I made them; on one occasion she overheard a conversation between me and my nephew, her grandson. I made a promised to give him some money for something he needed at the time, and he was ready for it. I'm sitting there listening to him baffled, trying my best to remember what I agreed to when my sister stepped in to save me from this embarrassment. "Mark, remember what I told you your aunt Sara would say when somebody asked her for something, and she would forget". I said what? She laughed and said first, you ask them, 'was I drunk when you asked me"? and when they say yes, you say, "well that's the problem".

I laugh when she told me and started quoting my aunt. But as I think about it now, what wasn't funny is that I quoted her so much that my nieces and nephews would say to each other "don't ask Uncle Mark to do nothing while he's drunk because you know he won't remember." My nieces were young when they started teasing me about that, the two youngest were aged somewhere around nine or ten years old, but what is sad and not funny, is that they still had reason to tease me about those words when they were fifteen and sixteen years old.

"Alcohol related dementia—is a type of alcohol related brain damage caused by regularly drinking too much alcohol over a period of years." (C.D.C.P)

There was a time when I thought alcohol did not hamper my ability to work; that I didn't lose focus, or brag to folks saying "yeah I'm an alcoholic but I'm not a drunk" and still make money, until 2018, that was the year my "walls of Jericho" came tumbling down.

By 2018, my lifestyle was drinking throughout the day and into the night, passing out, waking up, only to continue drinking. That was my norm, my routine, the way I lived and everyone who worked for me knew that, including my clients. I did not care if my workers knew, because I was their boss and I had the check book. But for my clients to know made a difference. However, there was no hiding it anymore. I looked the part and my alcoholism showed in the way I talked and walked. My bloodshot eyes with the watery glaze look. My slurred speech, and how I smelled, and because I was drinking so much, I had no appetite for food, therefore my weight loss was obvious. My complexion darken, and my skin was dry. I was unhealthy looking.

I didn't socialize so I had no woman in my life; didn't go out, not to visit, to gatherings or events, only to work. I had no decent clothes, but I did keep my body clean although I forgot how lotion felt.

The one thing I still had was my gift of gab, but it wasn't nearly as good as it once was.

The clients and customers I had were gone. My company folded. I had nothing left from the past, except my ability to advertise. It was the advertisement skills my mother taught me back during my teenage years, that maintain me and helped me to obtain a new client.

His company was in Israel. He was purchasing properties in bulk, in Detroit Michigan; and wanted me to manage, oversee the rehab and maintain them. Unfortunately, he did not know the flip side of that old saying, "what you don't know won't hurt you" well, dealing with me at that time gives it a different twist, "what you don't know will hurt you".

He entrusted me to evaluate and inform him if a property was worth investing in or not; I worked for him for a little over a year making somewhere between ten to fifteen thousand dollars per week before expenses. I had six full time employees and worked with four or five sub-contractors; and during that period, I never had to lift a hammer or pick up a nail; In addition to that, his company was doing business with a realtor who hired me to renovate and maintain their properties.

My Israel client allowed me to pick out any of their properties to live in, no rent, utilities or tax payments; in fact, they would pay me when that property needed repair. So now I ask you, who could have it better than that? With a layout like that, who could screw it up?

Let me answer that for you by name, Mark the drunk Jerome Holmes. I'll be even clearer "me, myself and I. How you ask? let me be brief:

A) Drinking in front of my workers equals no respect. Although some of them drink, my drinking all day, every day, and all the time, even to those that drank was too much.
B) "Alcohol Dementia" equals forgetting either to pay my workers or paying twice for the same work. They saw my weakness and took advantage of it.
C) Earning that kind of money with no physical labor, just driving from one place to another allowed me to drink

in the comfort of my car. I was under the air condition; always drunk.

D) Being drunk literally all the time equals not managing my day-to-day operations. Things are either not getting done or are being done wrong, and that equals my workers knowing that I'm too drunk to go and check on their work.

E) Drinking very early in the morning equals passing out at ten, or eleven o'clock in the morning, then waking up at one o'clock in the afternoon, thinking that it is the next day, that equals bad management.

F) Going to my client office to have a meeting or pick up money with bloodshot eyes smelling like alcohol equals, now they know why my work is behind or sloppy equals, the money slows down and then stops.

G) Drunk, and overpaying workers, wasting money, equals mismanagement of my client's money from Israel. This forced him to leave Israel and come to Detroit. He saw me looking like shit and his properties just sitting because I've done nothing to them. That equals no more money from Israel, equals you are fired, equals leave this house, equals that realtor you was working with because of the investor is no longer going to work with me, equals eviction, equals all my furniture thrown out on the curb when I'm not there, equals the neighbors taking it off the curb, equals I have less than I did before I started with them, equals the good times are over.

But what about the money in the bank? Here's a word of truth, a drunk doesn't save, we either give it away, get tricked out of it, spend it as fast as we get it or forget where we put it.

I was evicted and wasn't there when my furniture, appliances and clothes was set out on the curb; Several neighbors went on what could be described as a free for all, a frenzy, having their way at taking all my personal belongings. When they were done, not even a spoon or fork was left by the time I arrived; and worst of all, hidden in some of the furniture was thousands of dollars in cash I would stash away from time to time, so some received a double prize.

I spent 98% percent of the money in my bank account attempting a quick repair of the investor's properties. I previously lied to him saying that they were either repaired or being worked on, and although they weren't My goal was to make a good showing so he would not stop the flow of money. However, after all that spending the work couldn't catch up with the lie; so, I was fired, and had nothing.

You would think that would be enough to make any normal person stop drinking, smoking marijuana, and get their life together right, wrong. My love for alcohol was like the love a mother has for her child. Think about that. My constant losses, the distancing from those I have known for years, the endless lies, the Doctor's words, and still no change in me.

I was like a mother; the alcohol was like my child, and I was willing to die for it.

Now I have nothing but the dirty work clothes on my back, a toothbrush and a pair of worn-out paint splattered boots. My two cars were repossessed and the pickup truck I had needed an engine. Evicted, I'm living in the basement of a roach and rat-infested apartment building that belongs to an old client of mine who doesn't like me, and I don't like him.

Some years prior to that, I recall an appointment I had at my then doctor's office.

I remember being asked by the resident nurse after checking my blood pressure and finding it abnormally high, "Mr. Holmes, pausing between her thoughts, and with a concerned look, "why do you drink so much at a time?"

Sitting upright on the examination table I had no answer, nothing but this blank look on my face. I couldn't even come up with something that didn't make sense to say. Then she stepped closer looking me straight in my blood shot eyes having this non-understanding type of frown on her face "you seem to be a smart guy". Then dismissively turned and walked away holding her blood pressure device and tray in hand.

Her words will take a front row seat in my mind again, but it would be after some time into the future.

Thank you, God, that I was blessed with a mother who showed me how to be strong; thank you God, that I was bless with a mother who taught me survival. She taught me how to advertise, a lesson that has carried me throughout my adult life; Having this knowledge has always been the reason I could bounce back from difficult situations and get back on my feet. My mother taught me that "A bird in the hand is better than one in the bush". She defined the "bird" as knowledge, and with age, I have lived by that old saying. I had drunk myself into this unholy living arrangement and it will take the skills learned from her to bring me out.

The month was November, I remember it well because of "Thanksgiving"; while others was cleaning their homes in preparation for the holiday, I was cleaning that dungeon to keep the rats and roaches at bay. I would spray that asylum every night before I passed out, and even in my drunken and marijuana state of mind I only half slept, waking up constantly surveying the walls and looking at the foot edge of my bed, afraid that roaches would find their way next to my pillow crawling inside my ears and mouth, or a gang of rats may feel entitled to helping themselves to a shot or two of my liquor. But not even that could stop this love affair I had for liquor. I stayed to my routine, "stayed the course" as it's said, and refused to stop drinking.

I was in my third month there, and true to form finishing up what I had left in the bottle before I started my workday, thinking how this living arrangement has changed in my life. I had to accept it. Call it "cause and effect". My new reality. No longer did I have a house, a nice clean-living room where I could sit back in my big adjustable chair and watch my big screen TV. The days of sleeping in my king size bed were gone; Walking into my bright color kitchen; opening my well stock refrigerator for a snack was a thing of the past. While living at that apartment I refused to walk across the floor without socks and shoes on; I slept fully clothed and on guard afraid that a thief or loiterer may kick in the door and in a surprised panic do who knows what, after all, I was the only one living in that basement, and like always, "on my own".

Being in that position made me think crazy thoughts, and I couldn't blame getting drunk and high on anything or anyone other than myself. I chose to get drunk, and high, and what's crazier was sitting there complaining to myself about myself, eyes blurry from the marijuana and cigar smoke while having my way with the bottle of now cheap liquor. Imagine sitting there getting drunk mad at myself for getting drunk but hey, that is what addicts do. We are always looking for something or someone to blame, instead of "looking at the man in the mirror".

When I lived there, I never cooked, would never drink water from the kitchen faucet or turn the lights off, almost everything I once did before the eviction had faded into memory, nothing was the same, even my drinking. Well, the amount, anyway. Life for me was not good, not good at all. I was living day by day but still managed to drink, reduced to two and a half, three pints of cheaper liquor per day. I still managed to drink throughout the day and into the night; still smoked my weed mixed cigar chaser, and still passed out drunk and woke up right back at it.

I would shake my head in hidden shame, disgust, and full of [Self-Pity] about losing all that I had. Falling from having to have not, from money in pocket to turning in empty bottles; looking through my junk car for loose change, checking my clothes for any nickels or dimes I may have overlooked or missed. I went from loaning money to people who would ask me, to coming up with lies to borrow enough to feed my addiction. I was a mess and feeling [So Sorry for myself]. But I would not stop living that lifestyle. I would not stop drinking and smoking marijuana. Do you feel bad for me yet?

I was living in this man's basement for over three months at the mercy of doing whatever repairs he needed done; not only at that apartment building; he owned others. He paid me well below the normal cost; below minimum wage at times, in other words he paid me like I'm a drunk. I still had my pride, and was not going to reach out to others, because to ask meant telling the truth and no way would I expose what I had become, my addiction, or the circumstances caused by my self-destructive choices.

My self-esteem was low, but how people knew I lived before all this, allowed me to borrow twenty, and thirty dollars at times using lies like, "I left my wallet at home", or I'll go old school saying, "I'm waiting on a check to clear". My other lie I would use went, "I just finished up a job and the amount of money paid to me is larger than all the money I have in my bank account, so I have to deposit it and wait for it to clear". When the truth was that I had no bank account, and received no check; to be honest, if I were to get a check for what I was charging, it could be cashed at a dollar store and the seventy-five cents or one dollar that would be deducted for cashing it would be a major setback to my pockets.

My existence had become a lie. I was working hard for very little, but those twos and fews kept me afloat. I could buy a little food, but more importantly it gave me the money needed for my alcohol, cigars and marijuana abuse.

I still had transportation, nothing pretty, an old station wagon, but it enabled me to move around doing odd jobs here and there. Until one night in December, I'll never forget it because that was the night that proved I had no super ability to drive drunk and not get caught.

It was cold, wet and snowing; I was on my way to that dreadful basement. Driving drunk, I forgot to turn my car headlights on and out of nowhere, in my rear-view mirror was my worst nightmare.

I gave a double look and saw the police lights flashing behind me with no siren on but not making any attempt to go around my car. My body began to tighten up and sweat formed on my ball head dripping down my face. I thought to myself, no doubt this cop was coming for me. I knew I was in trouble for a number of reasons, starting with I had no driver license; an illegal license plate on the car, warrants for past tickets, no money, and breath stinking of alcohol.

The thought of trying to speed away in that junk car would push "dumb luck" to an unrealistic reality. So, I had only one choice to pull over, turned the car off and faced yet another situation my alcoholic choice has led me into.

"Driver license and registration sir" she asked while looking straight at me. I didn't want to turn my head toward her or say a word knowing that she would smell the liquor. "officer", speaking while my head is lowered toward the car floor. "I live two blocks that way", pointing to my left while holding my breath, trying to control my breathing and the smell coming out of my mouth. But when you drink as I did non-stop from dawn to dusk the smell of liquor becomes a part of you. It's like the color of my skin, impossible to rub off. But before I could tell her that I had no driver's license she asked "sir, have you been drinking?" I had no lie for this and responded yes, saying I just opened it because I'm going right down the street, again pointing to my left, "officer, I'm only two blocks away".

She asked me for my information again while slightly shaking her head in a disgusted manner. I continue, "I don't have a driver license, and this is the wrong license plate, but I have the title, but it's not transferred in my name yet". As I handed her the paperwork I continued, "officer one more thing, I have warrants for driving violation", she exhaled seemingly fed up with my talking, shook her head and with my paperwork in hand walked toward the patrol car.

The title wasn't transferred because I had accumulated so many tickets over previous years and not paid them, that the state of Michigan put me on a list of people not allowed to obtain license plates until these tickets were paid; at that time in Detroit Michigan, my violation debt was over six thousand dollars. I also had tickets in various suburbs and even one from the Michigan state highway patrol; On top of not paying them, I never showed up to a court hearing regarding them and accumulated over 50 bench warrants in the city and suburbs.

I was gripping my steering wheel with my sweaty palms waiting for her and her partner to walk back to my car to take me to jail. I thought to myself, I don't have anyone to call, and at that moment I was scared.

Twenty minutes seem like hours, and I had the worst feeling. I looked in my rear-view mirror and saw a tow truck moving closer to my car and the officers getting out of theirs calmly walking toward me. "Mr. Holmes, I could lock you up for all these tickets and warrants, you're out here driving drunk; your driver license suspended, and you don't look well, but I won't this time". I sat quietly listening, "what I'm going to do is confiscate this car and let you go". I was slightly relieved. She continued, "but Mr. Holmes, I don't know you, or what is going on in your life, but you need to get some help for yourself to deal with whatever is going on in your life", and with that said the two of them walked back to their car.

I took my tools out and was standing there on the curb of the sidewalk, it was dark; cold, nine maybe ten o'clock at night watching the only way I have managed to make money day to day being towed away, knowing that I can't get it back. Angry at myself but still full of self-pity, I walked away dragging my tools on the snow-covered sidewalk to that apartment building, sipping on the liquor she let me keep or more likely slipped her mind.

I arrived at the apartment drunk, sprayed it and passed out into a half sleep state; woke as usual three, four o'clock in the morning finishing off what I had left from the night before.

When eight o'clock arrived I was half drunk on the phone trying to get a ride to a small job I lined up the day before and was able to accomplish that. My ride was to pick me up at ten o'clock, so I could start working by ten thirty or eleven o'clock.

No longer mobile and without transportation I was unable to continue my morning drinking ritual. The liquor store was several blocks away and I was not walking in the cold. But as my head cleared, I decided to go online and advertise.

My method of advertisement was emailing flyers that outlined my construction skills to various real estate companies; That morning I sent out maybe twelve flyers to twelve companies in fifteen minutes; one company responded.

He asked me about my skills and how long I've been working on houses. I answered his questions; then he asked me if I could go to a property, price the repairs and call him from there saying "I want to get this property together as soon as possible".

Those words were music to my ears, and as my ride drove there, I celebrated this possibility while gobbling down on a pint of cheap alcohol.

I know what you're thinking, you're saying to yourself wow, what is wrong with this man? When is enough enough? or maybe you're questioning my mental state of mind.

An alcohol research center, in their report which is intitle "factors that cause alcohol abuse both internal and external" stated the following; as I read it while writing this book, I applied their findings to my life. let's start with "external":

A) Family Environment: I was one of many children in this country who grew up in a one parent home. However, my situation was that I did not know who my father was. That information was kept so tight from me that I didn't find out that I had a different father, until I was in my 40ties, and for that reason I can't speak on his history. But I was told that throughout my mother's life she would only drink a beer every now and then. In fact, throughout my childhood I never saw my mother drink alcohol. It was not a part of our household and beside her husband, my stepfather, she did not associate with drinkers, or people who would be considered alcoholic.

My stepfather was a functioning alcoholic during weekdays who drank heavily on the weekends. He had no major part in raising me or influence in my life.

What is funny about his story, is that he was considered to be and called by others an alcoholic.

I remember when I was about twenty-three, maybe twenty- four years old, my mother told me after the two of them returned from his doctor's appointment, that he was told that if he continued to drink, he would die; Amazingly this man completely stopped drinking alcohol that day, that very day. As I got older my life distanced me from him, but from time to time throughout the years I would run across him and have small talk; From what I could see, smell and was told by others he never went back to alcohol, never had another drink after that day he was told he would die. I respected that and would look at him and say to myself, now that is a man who wants to live.

I had five siblings, four older and one three years younger than me, and to my knowledge none of them had a history of abusing alcohol. However, a couple of them could be considered either crazy or damn fools, but that wasn't alcohol related, they just were.

B) Religion: my mother was deeply associated in Christian Faith, which is why alcohol, besides my stepfather was never seen, smelled or used in her home.

C) Education and Job Status: I graduated 12th grade; was taught skills that gave me the ability to make money, use common sense and stay independent. I've never had to deal with peer pressure, not as a kid, teenager or adult, so it's not that with me.

D) Age: well maybe if I add the research factor which is "Social and Culture Nature," then I could see a possible connection, because in my late teens I did hang around with older businesspeople, where drinking at lunches and dinner meetings was the norm, that is where I started drinking my alcohol "straight up" without a chaser as they did, so yes that had a slight impact but very slight.

I found more of a connection with the researchers "internal factors". let's start with:

A) "Drinking History": My response is no, because I didn't grow up around, nor was I in close association or deeply influenced by people involved with alcohol.

I feel that I created my own drinking history, which ties into the researcher's category "Personal choice". I fall into this category because even when I review their "Social and Culture" factor I realized that no one verbally encouraged me to drink, I had no peer pressure in school, no physical or mental abuse, and the only stressful situation I remember dealing with as a youth, was making my high-school football team, and drinking alcohol was not even a distance thought; as a young adult, well, you have to give me a minute, because I'm sitting here writing this book trying to think back of something, or some event in my life that would cause me to drink, and I honestly can't think of anything, even those business people I would meet with at the lunches and dinners, never encourage me to drink, everyone did their own thing. We didn't talk about alcohol, and no one held a gun to my head. Drinking alcohol was solely a decision made by me, therefore, my history with alcohol started with me and can only be ended by me.

B] Psychology Condition: Now this may be the answer to those of you asking yourself about my alcoholic actions, decisions, and mental state of mind. My choice to abuse alcohol has caused financial disasters, hospital visits, the endless lies to myself and people who care about me, but no matter the consequences which were always bad I continue to drink. So yes, I definitely fall in the category of having a psychological condition. However, the question I would have to ask myself is what kind of Psychological Category am I In? For example, some people drink because of depression; so, I will ask myself if I was depressed? looking back to the 80tis, my answer would be No, then how about the 90ties? again, I pause in thought, and again answer No. But the two thousands, would bring me to a different conclusion, especially the mid two thousands because through the 80ties and 90ties I was living a hidden lie with no reasons to expose my abuse to anyone I associated with. Most of them knew I drink, but not how much because at that time two factors were at play, #1: Although my alcohol drinking was gradually becoming a routine, it hadn't gotten out of control, yet. and #2: because when I lived in Cleveland, I was around lifetime friends and family, so my life was not isolated. I was not yet an antisocial person, but from 2000, especially 2005, living in Detroit away from all those I grew up and associated with, I no longer had to hide my abuse, my love ones could not reach out and touch me, and because being 300 miles away, a visit became a phone call and my hidden secrets became lies, so many that my life became a lie.

Living lies to the point of distancing myself from everyone I knew to protect the lies can and will cause depression, which will have a psychological effect on anyone.

I felt that pain inside but denied it, because we as people can lie so much that we will begin to believe them and therefore that lie becomes our reality.

In 2020, I had a conversation with my sister Joann, but before I spoke with her, I called a few friends in Ohio talking with them about me moving back to Cleveland. I had this sad story about wanting to be around people I know so when I die, people who care about me will know I am dead. However, I could feel that they were skeptical because of the lies in the past of me visiting there and was right to be. [It's called drunk talk, this happens when a person gets drunk and starts calling people they know, looking for pity. I call it pacifying self-pity or wanting sympathy for things you do. Some drunks will cry on the phone, while others talk endlessly about nothing. Me, I was never that type because I was always hiding my disease, but this one time I reached out looking for pity.

I was face to face with my sister Joann having this same conversation, and as I talked, she listened analyzing my words and facial expressions, then said "Mark maybe you should go there and visit first; then make up your mind to either move there permanently or not". She added "maybe you're just homesick, but you sound like you're depressed, asking me "Mark do you feel depressed"?

My sister didn't know about my many failures from alcohol abuse at that time, and I didn't tell her about me living in that apartment until after I moved out. She was among those I distanced myself from during that embarrassing period. We continue our conversation for about an hour and her words made me realize, that I was going through a depression, and that I was in denial of it; and although she didn't speak specifically about my drinking, I'm sure she knew alcohol was somehow involved in the conversation as well as the depression. But that's how she is, when you're grown, she won't speak on your personal issues, although she sees them, unless you do. She has two sayings when it comes to people's personal choices which are, "If you like It, I love It", or after listening to your story she'll say, "Nothing surprises me Mark, I am not surprised".

After speaking with the realtor, I arrived at his property around eleven o'clock, delaying my scheduled work until I finished with him; by twelve o'clock I was on the phone giving him a price on the repairs.

When I lost my Israel client, the work I was doing for people were small jobs making one, or two hundred dollars per job, keeping my price low although my labor was exhausting.

I priced low to make sure I would beat out any competition because my daily addictions were my life. I drank three pints of liquor per day continually throughout the day and into the night. Ten dollars per day spent on marijuana and was smoking no less than fifteen black & mild cigars per day at sixty-nine cents each; then factor in gas money and food. Add it up and I am ending my day with twenty or twenty-five dollars at the most. Then there was always work the guy whose basement I was living in needed, so basically unlike in my past when I would drink and pass out from the alcohol and marijuana, his demands double exhausted me.

One thousand seven hundred- and sixty-five-dollars labor cost, and the realtor supplied the materials. This work would take me two days to complete working non-stop from 8am to 6pm.

It was early February on a Tuesday morning when the realtor gave me a cash deposit of five hundred dollars. I hadn't held five hundred dollars at one time in over three months. I thought to myself, finally, my God, finally; and the best benefit to this was that his company had a lot more work for me at this price or better to come. I celebrated this blessing from God, by killing myself drinking more alcohol.

Thursday morning came and I was finished with the work receiving twelve hundred dollars in my hand, and after I got it, I was on my way to another property the realtor wants done.

The repairs on this new job would cost two thousand three hundred dollars; He agreed and gave me a one-thousand-dollar labor deposit and with a bottle of liquor in hand I was on my way to a car lot.

I started that job on a Saturday, and after two days working non-stop, I received my pay from that. I was now driving my own truck, had money in my pocket and working my way back to living a decent life.

Monday afternoon, two days after I started the second job the realtor asked me to meet him at a different house because he wanted to talk with me, so while driving, I filled my mouth with big red chewing gum to cover the alcohol smell. I arrived; went inside and as we walked through the house he asked me, "Mark do you own the house you live in?" I had never discussed my living arrangements with him and was surprised by the question. Responding "funny you ask me that because I'm looking for a place to stay;" That is when he said "Mark all the utilities are on at this house, and I tell you what, I won't charge you a security deposit if you want this house, but you have to do the repairs so if you want it, it's yours. You pay me seven hundred dollars per month". I agreed and he handed me the keys. as he pulled off my head was spinning, I thought to myself, I can't believe this is happening; quietly excited I thought now, finally, I am out of that basement and away from that tyrant.

That same day, I cleaned the house from head to toe; then drove from there to the first U-Haul lot I saw, and from there to that hell hole grabbing my bed, tv, and the rags I called clothes headed to my new house, with, of course, a bottle in hand, celebrating the entire way.

So now you're wondering, did he at any time say to himself, that the drinking has to stop? Or if I ever thought about all those losses? Did I ever think to myself that never again would I put myself in the position I just got out of?

I'll answer those questions for you. Yes! I did give thought to those things and yes, I did say to myself that I would never put myself back into what I just got out off? And with that said, I know what you're thinking, Did I mean any of it? I'll answer that too, No! I didn't mean a word In fact, as my work and money increased with this company so did my drinking, marijuana and black and mild use.

After a couple of months my income went from twenty-five dollars at the end of a day, to twenty-five hundred dollars minimum profit per week, after paying whoever I would use to help me with certain jobs, I was pocketing a minimum of eighteen hundred dollars.

I was living again, so I thought, It took me one week to rehab the house I was living in, and within four months I worked out a deal with the realtor and purchased the property. My income increased, so I bought myself a nice pickup truck, a s.u.v, brand new furniture that included a big comfortable reclining chair, and a big screen TV.

I had AC units and cable TV, all the things I needed to make my home life as comfortable as possible, because once I got off work and stumbled inside my house, I wasn't going anywhere. My old routine was back in rare form; the drinking was back, four to five pints per day drinking all day, the marijuana went back to a half ounce or more per week and my black & mild use increased to 25 maybe 30 cigars per day, until I passed out.

Just think about it, from that humble February, when I first received that realtor phone call 2019, to September 2020, my life was good, money being made, alcohol being drank, weed and black & mild being smoked; and I still wasn't receiving phone calls from people who cared about me, so I didn't have to lie, life was good, and at this point I was completely an antisocial person. My life consisted of four things, work, alcohol, marijuana and black & miles.

I had it made Hun? Really Mark?

Well let's look at my good life with sober eyes for a moment; let's analyze it with questions for a moment; for a moment let me ask myself this, what benefits did I gain from drinking alcohol?

Answer:

A) by drinking alcohol the way I was, I was able to accomplish ahh, ahh
B) well, I ahh ahh.
C) ------------- ahh.

Ok, before that becomes too embarrassing let's flip the question: by drinking alcohol what loss did I obtain?

Answer:

A) I lost houses, three of them last count. Cars got repossessed several of them. I lost a lot of money and business clients. I lost respect from past employees, and people I knew. I was embarrassed in front of all my neighbors with that eviction. I had no decent clothes and stopped buying lotion. I went from having bad relationships with women to no relationships, and because of all the alcohol I was drinking I lost my sex drive and the desire for one. And even if I'd found a woman willing to have sex with me, she would have to be able to put up with the alcohol smell coming from my body and overcome the liquor smell from my breath. And if she could do that, it still wouldn't happen, because drinking all that alcohol, had my body so messed up that I couldn't get an erection watching a porn flick.

But that was my so-called good life, and I was living it just the way I wanted, until late September, that was when all those past years of alcohol and drug abuse finally caught up with my health.

According to the "CDCP "alcohol abuse causes a weakened blood flow to the heart". "It can cause an irregular heartbeat, sharp chest pains, and shortness in breathing".

late September 2020, for the third time in my life I started feeling those familiar chest pains, but this pain was different. Earlier, I told you about the chest pain I felt in 2017, but back then the pain had a tightness like a vice to my chest. This time in addition to that, I felt a crushing pressure like a squeezing sensation rapidly tightening, causing me to sweat uncontrollably. I repeated what I did back then; put the bottle down and sat still in my chair, breathing light trying not to move a muscle; and after about ten minutes the pain eased, but although my chest felt sore, I would resume my smoking and drinking.

Throughout the month, the pain would come without warning, not every day but enough to where I expected it. But I would continue my routine anyway, only now waiting for it, making this horror a part of my ritual.

End of September 2020, I can't specifically remember the day the pain started again, but like I said it came and went as it chose to, picking it's time to come. This went on and into October. At first this pain would last for short periods of time; each time leaving what felt like an inner scar, unseen on the outside of my body. But by November it changed, feeling as if it was moving across my chest weighing heavy, and close to my heart, lasting for longer periods of time, and in addition to that, my breathing was being affected; my sitting still tactic was not working as it did before. So, to ease it, I would have to slump over and slowly twist my body from left to right; up and down slowly for fifteen, twenty minutes, before the pain would ease, and my breathing would return to somewhat normal.

But not even that would make me slow down or stop drinking. I wasn't even sure if what I was doing was actually working, all I knew is that at that moment it helped ease the symptoms.

I use the word symptom, because I knew that these things my body was going through were leading to something, something big. But some part of me was accepting this, wanted to accept it, almost like suicide or something.

I was alone, and I made myself that way, I was a marijuana head, an alcoholic and I made myself that. I was a liar living a lie and I did that. I had material things, new clothes, shoes, jewelry, but never wore them because I never went out, nice vehicles that I would drive when I took a day or two off work, but I only drove them to the liquor store or laundry then back home. When I think about it the only thing that kept me going was my work. That became my only reason, it was my life, and now that I think about it right now as I write, I realized that I was depressed. As I write this, I now realize that my alcohol abuse had become my way of dealing with my depressed state of mind. I didn't realize that until now. I allowed these symptoms to go on because I was suicidal. I didn't realize that until now. I was depressed from being depressed, and I did that to myself. I had my hand painfully in a jar, selfishly holding on to a bottle accepting the hardship, when all I had to do was to let the bottle go slide my hand out, and all the pain would go away.

I had finalized what I wanted to say in this book a week ago and was spending this time rewriting parts of it so that my words would be clear.

I did not intend to write what I just said about suicide, that portion was not initially written because I had not thought about it until now and as I rewrite parts in this book, I won't edit that part. Up until this minute I did not know the power of denial but now, as of right now I do, I mentioned denial in this book earlier but didn't realize just how deep I suffered from it until this moment. Denial can be dangerously scary.

November brought on more intense pain and breathing issues, and by December there would be times my heart would be pumping so hard that when I stood up the dizziness would force me to the floor; That is when I decided to go to the doctor's office.

The next morning, I finished the alcohol from the night before, chewed a big red bubble gum and walked into the doctor's office. After my examination, there was what seemed to be a minor panic as the nurse called out for the doctor and stepped into the hallway with my blood pressure results in hand.

The doctor came into the room and asked, "Mr. Holmes how do you feel"? My head spinning and drunk I lied, fine; then he continued, "Mr. Holmes, I am asking because your blood pressure is extremely high and I'm thinking about admitting you into the hospital, can you tell me why you think this is"? I was sitting there still drunk from drinking in the parking lot. I looked over at him unable to think of a quick suitable lie, so admitted that I had been drinking alcohol in the parking lot right before I came in; he responded, "yes, I can smell it Mr. Holmes". He continued, "would you like to stop drinking?" But before I could respond he continued, "I can refer you to various programs". Of course, I lied, yes. He gave me another appointment along with literature and a prescription.

I stumbled out of the office, got into my truck, and finished the liquor I started before entering his office, drinking as I drove to the pharmacy.

When I received the medication, I promptly read the label that said, "Do Not Drink Alcohol While Taking." I went home, put those pills in my cabinet and never looked at them again.

Celebrating my getting through that visit, by opening a fresh pint, purchased while on my way home.

No risk was going to be taken for my second doctor's appointment, so no drinking after I woke up from passing out that morning. I even managed to eat a sandwich on my way there, and with a mouth full of breath fresheners, I arrived at 9 am. My goal was to get in, and out as fast as possible so that I could resume my routine. At this appointment, I was told that my blood pressure was high but not as before. The Doctor handed me a prescription this time to see the Doctors at a hospital, for a test on my heart, stomach pain, and dizziness, which I started having frequently.

The Doctor at the hospital wrote me several prescriptions, for headaches, high blood pressure, and chest pain, but again after reading the labels that said, "No Drinking Alcohol While Taking This Medication" they went on the same shelf as the others making a new home for the spiders.

The moment I put those medications on my shelf, was when I decided to die before I would give up alcohol and drug abuse. I was not in denial when I made that decision and was fully aware that I am an alcoholic and drug addict. I would often use words like, when I die to others.

At this point in my life, there was no communication with anyone outside of my work. No friends, no family, and no associations, not even with my son. My theme in life was a title from a famous rapper album called, "Ready to Die".

There were no more doctor appointments made, no concern from me regarding my health, and my drinking routine was completely how I lived my life.

By February 2021, my addictions started to manifest itself in my work; like before, I started slacking, not getting things done and falling behind. My income, which was now roughly four thousand dollars per week, began to decrease, and the realtor, like the previous clients I had screwed up with, started asking me questions.

My chest pains, and breathing had gotten so bad that before I passed out sleep, I would set my cell phone on 911, and unlock my front door so that the ambulance medics could have easy access. I was on the pathway to death, but stupidly, selfishly, convinced myself that I wasn't afraid to die. My fear was, to be sitting in that chair dead for weeks rotting away with no one ever finding out.

February 25th, 2021, around midnight, I was sitting in that chair drunk, looking at a program about black men, and women, who fought for the freedom of blacks, and died for the rights we as blacks have now, but on this night, I did not pass out. I just sat there looking at the TV but not watching it, hearing the sound but not listening; my mind was thinking back on my life and the people in it.

I was having thoughts of my mother, who passed away in the late 80s, thinking, if she would momentarily come back to life and stood in front of me, how disgusted she would be, asking "Why Mark." As my eyes teared up, I said in a whisper, what could I possibly say to this woman, who thought the world of me. Then the words of Mrs. Lewis, the mother of my second family, shaking her head "um um um Mark, you don't get it". My mind continues this journey into the past, thinking about those who had wished misfortune for me, and how they would laugh at what I've become. A liar, coward, so selfish and stupid, if they could see me now, how they would shake their head in a pleasant disgust. In my mind, I could hear some say I told you so, Mark isn't all that smart, while others say Mark, you are better than this.

As I closed my eyes and lower my head, I could hear those who have always cared about me, the ones I avoided, lied too, and pushed away. Nina words from decades ago saying "Mark, what is wrong with you" and I could feel the words of past associates saying, "man you need to stop playing with yourself, and, Mark, you're gone do what you want to do anyway, what's the holdup either do it or don't", and Lewis who would simply put it this way, "So Mark, you have decided to die and to you that's ok", he would calmly continue, "well if that's your decisions then I guess it's ok, just keep me out of it".

Their words and others, screamed in my head yelling inside my ears, saying "Mark, don't nobody have to tell you, you know what you have to do".

These things that was once said to me found its was deep inside my head, ringing loudly, as they repeated over and over again, drowning out the headache and dizziness, taking away my desire to lift that bottle to my mouth.

This went on for three nights; two of them continuing during the day as I worked, and as they continued, I could not drink alcohol, and during those evenings when I'd sipped, a feeling of guilt and weakness would overwhelm me. It's unexplainable, I felt like I was hiding from something, or that people whose voices I was hearing was looking at me, I don't know! I felt ashamed and dirty. Then I did something I hadn't done in decades, I talked with God about it, not on my knees, No bowhead, or prayer, just a conversation. We just talked, and after the conversation, the liquor I had left went down the toilet.

Later that night, while still thinking about that conversation, it hit me, after all those years it finally happened, I got sick of myself, disgustingly mentally sick, and felt fed up and tired of being stupid. I felt dirty, pitiful, just pathetic. I felt like the words of that song, "tired of being tired".

Although my drinking had lessened, the weed and cigar smoking, the chest pains, short breathing, headaches and dizziness continued through the rest of February 2021, but intensified as March set in.

On March 1rst, I woke up around 4:35 that morning, turned over and looked at an almost full bottle of liquor and for the first time in over twenty years, I turned my body in the opposite direction and left it untouched.

I fully woke up at eight o'clock in the morning, and for the first time in 2 years, turned the light on in my bathroom, and took a real honest look at "The man in the mirror".

I had not woken up sober in many years, usually I would keep the bathroom light off, not wanting to look at my glazed blood shot eyes and how skinny I was. But this time I did.

I got dressed, and left out but on this day, drove past the liquor stores, and reintroduced myself to what is called breakfast. I pulled into the parking lot and called in an order of beacon, eggs with cheese and wheat toast, and I did drink, only this time, orange juice replaced the alcohol.

I picked up my food, ate with the biggest smile on my face and started my workday. I felt like I won a battle, and I did that night, and that morning, but that was one battle, not the war.

That day was hard, a mental battle fighting my routine and habits built from years of alcohol abuse, but that day was spent sober and for the first time in decades, my workday ended at 8:45pm. As I drove, I was at in ahh, literally, because I could not remember the last time I saw the sun set.

I drove past the liquor stores to my house, went inside and sat in my chair but could not go to sleep. I was up all night, and into the morning sitting in that chair while my mind raced with those previous thoughts of people from my past.

I was never a person who liked the taste of alcohol, it was nasty tasting to me, really. Even when I was a young man and would take women out to dinner, I would order red wine, "zinfandel", but only for show. Honestly, I could never drink alcohol with food, and would always order a soda alongside.

I could not drink beer, and not even my beloved brandy with food. I just didn't like the taste. My drinking was for one purpose, to get drunk and believe me, there was nothing classy about my addiction.

The morning of March 2nd, was like the day before, spent without alcohol. The previous night, I must have dozed off in my chair at some point, because when I woke up it was seven o'clock in the morning. But I do remember walking into my bedroom and looking at that same bottle and leaving it where it sat.

That morning, I went into the bathroom, turned the light on, and although I still didn't like what I saw, got dressed: stopped at a restaurant, ate breakfast, and worked free of alcohol, and once home I went to sleep around 10pm, and slept until 7am.

March 3rd, 2021. The reason that morning was significant, is because that is the morning I threw the bottle of liquor away, and what makes that action so relevant, is because that act triggered the first day of positive change in my life.

As I worked, suddenly, I started feeling sick; It happened without warning, feeling drained; having no energy, my body felt tired.

I literally could not lift 50 pounds, and as my body weakened, I sat down wondering what was going on with me.

This was not chest pain, or shortness of breath; not a headache or dizziness but something different that forced me to go home. I figured that this feeling may be from my lack of sleep or something and began to get concern. Talking to myself "maybe when I eat, and get some rest, tomorrow I will feel better. As I drove home, I could feel my body getting weaker and weaker.

Finally, I made it; walked inside my house, sat down and started feeling a cold sensation, very cold inside, and weak.

I went into my bedroom; grabbed a blanket then walked back to my living room chair; As soon as I covered my body with the blanket, my body started getting hot, hot to the point of sweating; Now I'm getting concerned, wondering if I could have the Coronavirus, so I called this guy I knew who once had it and told him about the things my body was going through, asking, if he had these symptoms when he had the Coronavirus, but after explaining my concerns to him, he responded "hey Mark hold that thought, I'll call you right back"; but while waiting I started shaking, then shivering as I sat there, feeling weaker. Dozing off and on, I decided to go to bed. Sleep must have come about nine o'clock that night.

I woke up about seven in the morning laying in a puddle of sweat that reaped the smell of alcohol, and that's when it hit me, that I'm going through "Detox.

No work for me that day, still feeling sick, I must have sweated off five pounds of pure liquor, and March 4th, repeated March 3rd.

On the morning of March 5th, I felt a little better, but still had no appetite for food, because for years, smoking marijuana dictated that.

I knew that I had marijuana in my hallway closet, and walked over; pulled out the last bag; took out a cigar and started mixing it in the tobacco, but before finishing the mix I stopped; that conversation I had with God, came back to mind; followed by the guilt, and the feeling of being mentally weak, I said to myself out loud, "man no, and what followed was Nina's words in my mind, all loud, "Mark

What Is Wrong With You!" So, I decided to let my appetite happen naturally and I threw the bag of marijuana away.

I had never experienced "detoxification, "[aka detox]." I only saw it on television programs or a movie about some person going through the shakes, holding their stomach, throwing up and stuff. I didn't have it as bad as I've saw it, but I had it. Mine lasted for three days, and during that drama, I couldn't eat, drink water, or use the bathroom, not number one, or two. I guess my waste was coming out of my pores. But when I woke up on that fourth day, my bed was dry and I was hungry, thirsty, and on top of that, my bowel movement was back. It was a dark red, black and green in color looking like black mold and the smell was unbearable. It reaped of alcohol, smelling like spoiled rotten food coming out of me.

But when I got off the toilet, I felt like I just got baptized; showered and ate nearly half of the food in my refrigerator; I couldn't get enough water.

March 3rd, 2021, will be a day I will remember for the rest of my life. It was the day I mentally and physically started my fight for sobriety. But there are those who would say, why are you writing a book now? It hasn't been long enough for you to be giving advice or even claiming victory over drugs and alcoholism; That I should wait three, five or ten years to talk about this.

I'll respond to them this way. This is my story, about one of several battles I've had to fight throughout my life, and after 38 years of living this failed lifestyle that almost killed me on several occasions, it will not take me three, five or ten years to know that I will never return to that.

Alcohol, like cocaine, crack, pcp, and marijuana, isn't the big bad wolf, not to me. These things do not have the power of persuasion, they can't physically talk to you, or whisper sweet nothings in your ear. They do not have physical power to force itself on you. Drugs and Alcohol do not have legs, it can't walk to your house or apartment and kick down your door, and definitely can't hold a gun to your head.

We make a choice either to use it, or not, and depending on that choice we must either find a place to buy it, put ourselves where it is, or allow someone involved with it into our lives, or not. But it all comes down to decisions, and choices we make. Dope and Alcohol is a substance that just sits there until we decide to either pick it up or walk away.

I have been very stupid for a very long time, and now I chose not to be stupid anymore, Now I chose to live, I don't feel like dying. Now I chose to buy a good dinner, instead of so-called good marijuana. Clothes instead of alcohol; Now I choose a sociable lifestyle with friends and family, over an anti-social one.

I don't know how you feel about your life, but these days I feel good about mine. I feel clean and fresh, I feel strong and confident. I can speak the truth instead of living a lie. My mind is clear, not clouded and I don't want a shot of liquor, I prefer a glass of water. I don't feel like smoking marijuana because I don't want to.

Quitting my use of alcohol and marijuana was not the end of that fight, only the beginning, and these days I don't wake up or go to sleep fearing my future; I go to sleep and wake up living for my future. When you've been down that dark path for so many years, it takes determination not to go back; It takes inner strength and belief in yourself. This Is an issue of self-esteem.

When you look in the mirror can you honestly say that you like what is looking back?

Self-denial is strong and easy to acquire because it allows us to stay weak, even in the face of death.

If I'm going to kill myself, it's not going to be with a bag of weed or a bottle of liquor. I'm not going out that way. I don't want to die, so I am not going to let something I can control take me out that way. I prefer natural causes from old age. I can't control that, but what I can do is live an active, meaningful existence, going places, seeing things, spending time with family, barbecue, parks, restaurants, and concerts, you know, living life, so when it is my time to go, I'll go like that…not drunk or high living in the box that drugs and alcohol puts you in. But Living, Because Life is bigger than that.

I don't hate cocaine, but I know the effect it can have on me, so I don't mess with it.

I don't hate crack cocaine, but I know the effect it can have on me, so I don't mess with it.

I don't hate marijuana, like I don't hate slick fast talking women, but I know the effect it can have on me, so I don't mess with it.

I'm not scared of alcohol and don't have any hate for it, but I know the effect it has had on me, so I don't mess with it.

and so I'll say this to those who say to me that maybe I should wait three, five or ten years before I speak about my fight with those substances, that as I continue in my fight against drugs and alcohol, and as I live this new freedom I've chosen, I do not exactly know all the things that I'm going to do with the rest of my life, but I know exactly what I'm not going to do and that is, No More Drugs, and Alcohol.

(Ps, since I wrote this book, It seems like It has been years of freedom from alcohol and drugs. I don't even count anymore.)

About the Author

I appreciate you taking time out of your life to read about the craziness that was in mine.

I can't describe it as exciting or wild, and to use the expression "those were the days" could be taken the wrong way because that expression is usually said when people are reminded of events, or situations with a smile, and would use the full expression "Those were the good old days."

However, my life back then, the decisions I made, and actions I took were not ones that made me smile, nor do I consider them "the good old days." If I were to sum up my life and lifestyle back then, the word would be sad; therefore, "those were sad times."

If you were to ask me why I wrote this book and what was my goal, my answers are simple. I wanted my friends and family to know what I've been through. I had no goal of writing about my life and taking this to a publishing company. It was not my idea for the general public to see or know about my addictions, just those who I hurt, lied to, distanced myself from, my friends, and family.

When I grab a pencil and paper, my original thoughts were to write a letter explaining where I've been and what I have been doing and, when I finished, to personally hand-deliver it to them. But once I started explaining, and most of them I grew up with, I just kept writing and writing. Then weeks later, after twenty-one years, I finally went to Cleveland, Ohio, to visit as many of them I could.

I gave the first copy to a close friend of mine whom I had been lying to for years because I was afraid to verbally start that conversation. She read it, asked me questions about my words in relation to our friendship, and then said, "Mark, you should finish this. It can help a lot of people!" So I finished it.

My second goal was to somehow donate it to AA and NA groups. After my sister read it. She advised, "Mark, if you want to reach a lot of people, find a publisher. They'll reach the people." So I did, and here we are.

I love my life now. There is no feeling better than this freedom from alcohol and marijuana; to wake up and go to sleep in my right mind, to spend my money on food and clothes; going out listening to music, festivals, and just being out—this feeling, living in this type of freedom, instead of the box or cage addictions keep you in is a feeling a difference. I mean, wow, it's just a beautiful thing. Please do not die from that without experiencing this.

Lightning Source UK Ltd.
Milton Keynes UK
UKHW010815090223
416681UK00002B/475